I'LL BEAT YOU TO THE CORNER

In loving memory of Dougie

CHUCK HUBBELL

I'll Beat You to the Corner
Copyright © 2021 by Chuck Hubbell

All rights reserved. No part of this publication may be reproduced, distributed, or transmitted in any form or by any means, including photocopying, recording, or other electronic or mechanical methods, without the prior written permission of the author, except in the case of brief quotations embodied in critical reviews and certain other non-commercial uses permitted by copyright law.

ISBN
978-1-956161-21-2 (Hardcover)
978-1-956161-20-5 (Paperback)
978-1-956161-19-9 (eBook)

TABLE OF CONTENTS

Introduction vi

The Past that Happened Today 1
Building Cities 5
School Days 9
The Box Babysitter 11
Boys Will Be Boys 15
Art Class 19
A Change in the Air 23
The Prolonged Change 25
High Anxiety 29
Dougie's Mother at School 33
The Monsters Are Here! Run! 35
The Final Race 37
The Horse Is Out of the Barn 39
Marching for Dimes 41
Rotary, Mom and Dougie 43
My Epiphany 47
Dougie Is Alive 49

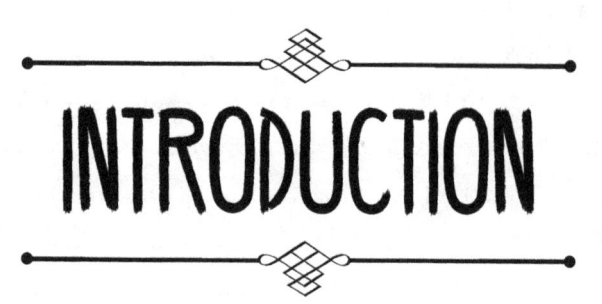

INTRODUCTION

IT IS A MARVELOUS WONDER of our very creation, and at the very same time, it is extremely interesting how a smell, song, photo, or vision can trigger several deeply buried memories.

In the book, *The Holographic Universe,* the author, Michael Talbot, talked about his journey to find where the brain stores our memory. Among other things, his quest involved the pursuit of learning exactly how we can see a photo of someone that we haven't seen in forty years and still know immediately who it is in the photo.

The same is true with our other senses. Perhaps, Psalm 139 really tells it exactly the way God intended for it to be for all to learn: "For I am fearfully and wonderfully made." With all the scientific research that has been completed on the subject, I prefer to think that God knew exactly what He was doing, and, I am quite content in being able to believe exactly that.

THE PAST THAT HAPPENED TODAY

THE AUTUMN AFTERNOON WAS RIPE with a gorgeous blue sky, complete with an abundance of cirrus clouds. As I was sitting on the porch swing, my attention was drawn toward two young boys. They seemed to be about seven years old and were moving dirt with a purpose only given to boys their age. They were creating roads… and building cities. The yellow trucks, bull dozer and frontend loader brought it all back to me in a torrent of memories and an overwhelming wave of emotion.

My life had crossed over into the world of real life make-believe. When I was their age, in the middle of the twentieth century, I was a living testament—how things were a part of a different time and a different place. *"What are little girls made of? Sugar and spice and all things nice. That's what little girls are made of. What are little boys made of? Snips and snails, and puppy dog tails. That's what little boys are made of."*

There was a difference between the way boys and girls played. Princes and fairy tales would not rule the day for the young boys; instead, they were eager to build. Tadpoles and frogs were used to entice and scare girls who were hoping to kiss a frog that would become their prince, and they would live happily ever after.

They call us "baby boomers." We were born after the Second World War and the Korean War. Returning war heroes helped stimulate Economic growth in a way that had never been seen before. In turn, an abundance of new houses were built in new subdivisions. People every-where seemed to be on the move.

My family was no exception. My Father and Mother participated in the relocation boom of Boomers. As a young couple, they had a baby girl who was born just a year before their second child was born. The honor of being that second child fell to me. A boy, yes, a young boy with all boy tendencies. They had a third child that died tragically of SIDS and another boy who was born four years later. Despite all of my wishes, he was never old enough to be involved and interact with good old number two. By the time I would turn seven, my mother lost another baby girl to Sudden Infant Death Syndrome, SIDS. Yet Again, my parents were expecting another child, and we needed a new place to live.

That place was in a new subdivision, with mounds of fresh dirt in which a boy could get lost. Except for the different colors, the side by side two story duplexes all looked the same. Each unit was just like the next. To this day, each time I play Monopoly and gaze upon the red "hotel" pieces, I remember the houses that looked like boxes. Pete Seeger's song said more about where we moved than I ever could:

"Little boxes on the hillside
Little boxes made of ticky tacky
Little boxes
Little boxes
Little boxes all the same
There's a green one and a pink one and a blue one and a yellow one
And they're all made out of ticky tacky
And they all look just the same."

BUILDING CITIES

LOOKING BACK, IT SURE SEEMS like the move was planned by forces beyond the control of our young family. We moved into a house that looked like a blue box, but each end was part of a duplex and had a separate dwelling. Within a week, another family had moved next door. They had a boy and a younger girl…yuck. The little boy's name was Dougie, and it didn't take very long to learn that we were the same age. As our first encounter began, Dougie dropped what he was carrying and said, "I'll beat you to the corner." "On your mark, get set, go!" He started to run as he got the last word out, and I began to chase him. He won what would become the first of many races to the corner. I had vowed to beat him next time. "I'll beat you to the corner" was our invitation to drop everything we were doing and race to the corner. "On your mark, get set, go," and with those words, it was official. Over the next several months, we raced countless times. He won several times, and fortune allowed me to beat him to the corner several times.

Back to moving day they continued to unload their possessions, I watched with great interest as they unloaded and unpacked some yellow metal toys that had originally been in a bigger box. My yellow toys had the same look, but they were different; however, they were still about the same size. He had a bulldozer and a steam shovel. They were the perfect complement to my dump truck and front-end loader.

The fresh black topsoil could be a curse when it rained, but it was a road paving nirvana to two boys who were bent on building new cities and a whole new world.

We built roads for hours. We graded roads, and we moved dirt as our imaginary cities grew into places where people could live and work. We made places for stores and factories. We shared the same mindset, and there was no dissention between us. We didn't need a foreman. If the road didn't seem right, we would simply do it all over again. If weather washed away the roads, we were ready to rebuild. It was easy to say that finer roads have never been built. Any disagreements were settled with a race to the corner.

We were two boys—the same age, the same size, and the same temperament—riding the same school bus and attending the same school. Life doesn't get any better than that.

Somewhere along the way, boys that age learn to remove their shirts when they played outside. When Dougie and I did remove our shirts, it soon became blurred as to which shirt belonged to whom. Our mothers did not seem to mind as long as we each ended up with a shirt at the end of the day.

Soon, our idyllic life blossomed into, "Can Dougie eat supper with us?" Sometimes, it was the other way around. Both of us ate the same food, and it was always at one another's house.

SCHOOL DAYS

THE SCHOOL BUS STOP WAS at the corner. Every morning, our day started just the same. As we left our dwellings in the blue box, one of us would let out a robust "On your mark, get set, go!" With those words, our day had officially started. The winner was rewarded with the window seat. School was mostly unremark-able. We labored through addition, subtraction, and of course, cursive writing. We both had the same routine when we returned home on the yellow school bus. First, a snack was in order. Then, it was time for the day's homework, and it had to be completed before we could go out to build. Looking back, it is easy to understand why our mothers did not allow us to do homework together. If we had, we surely would have ended up with the same grades. When the homework was completed and the work approved by our Moms, we changed our clothes, and we were off to build.

THE BOX BABYSITTER

TELEVISION (TV) PROGRAMS WERE IN black and white, and we just marveled as we watched one of the three available stations. When we watched TV, it involved the same routine. We would turn on the TV and wait 25 seconds. Then, we would watch as a picture would appear from a dot; it was a sight to behold. We had a choice between channel 2, 5 or 7, and each channel was assigned to its respective network: CBS, NBC, or ABC. Pick your poison. The screen was small, but the TV set took up a lot of space. Equipped with a ball on top, the TV had two extendable rods and its own base that had to be moved and adjusted whenever the channel was changed.

Although TV existed, it was reserved for Saturday morning cartoon baby-sitting. Can you say, "What's up Doc?" Saturday became the day the when parents slept in, and we could not build until they were awake. The reason probably was a result of all the noise those heavy pieces of equipment made as they pushed dirt, built cities, and belched the clouds of pretend black smoke.

Dougie and I were allowed to watch TV when it rained. The available programming introduced us to a whole new world, including a flying man with X-ray vision. With the twist of the dial, the scenery could change. At once, we were immersed into the world of horses and cowboys and Indians. There was even a cowboy hero who could fly an airplane. Another twist of the knob introduced us to Howdy Doody or Bozo the clown, and we shared in their antics as we watched. We knew the stuff wasn't real, but that was sometimes difficult to remember, especially when we were exposed to monsters that were placed on earth to harm all of us…one child at a time. With one eye closed, we watched the scary monsters in total captivation.

BOYS WILL BE BOYS

AT SCHOOL, OUR RECESS PROVIDED a time when all the boys recounted the antics of the latest monster from the tube. A favorite antic involved throwing our arms over our heads and making the ever popular "grrrrr" sound. When the girls screamed, we were delighted with our success. We all laughed a lot when the girls ran, and it provided us with great fun. If one of us could throw in a frog or a wooly worm, well, it just didn't get any better than that.

Through programs on the TV or with encouragement of our parents, we learned the typical boy things. We arm wrestled, thumb wrestled, and leg wrestled. Each encounter usually produced a decisive winner. It was a time of being a winner or loser. They didn't give out trophies for participation. Being a winner or being a loser defined who you were. Puppies did the same thing. One puppy would win a skirmish and then lose another. Just as in life, the winner is rewarded with a brief moment of celebration until the next encounter. Later in life, I enjoyed a career in sales, and it was there that I learned an important lesson; we are only as good as our next sale.

That was the time in our lives when we learned that boys don't cry, and if we did cry, we discovered that we were very vulnerable to the bullies among us. From that important lesson, we leaned another one. We figured out that two strands of rope were stronger than one, and two boys could stand up to the bully better than one. Once, I arm wrestled the schoolyard bully, and everyone was in awe when I won.

Recess was also a time spent avoiding girls and having each other's back should the bully choose to pick on either of us. Wild horses and bullies couldn't tear us apart. The bullies tried but the horses not so much.

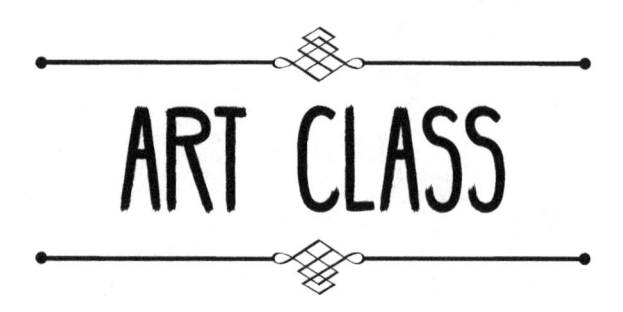

ART CLASS

ALTHOUGH SCHOOL WAS UNREMARKABLE, ART soon became my favorite way to spend time during the school day. I paid the most attention when I was creating art. The teacher was skilled in developing our creative "expertise". We were in a different room; instead of the usual desks and chairs, there were easels and tables. We could create art, and we were even allowed some talking in class during that time period. There was chalk, paint, clay, colored pencils, and big sheets of paper all for us. We had no idea who Leonardo Da Vinci, Rembrandt, and Vincent Van Gogh were, but we became them in our own minds. I was a burgeoning artist, and I loved absolutely everything about art; however, my budding art career ended very abruptly when a couple of well-intentioned statements destroyed what I thought I was capable of becoming.

My teacher was the encourager-in-chief, and she did her best to motivate us. I still remember that day; I was so excited! I had created a masterpiece, and she even described my masterpiece as "very interesting". Wow! My buttons were busting, and my hat was too small. As I ran from the school bus that day, I couldn't wait to get home and tell my mother. I was so proud, and I knew she also would be beaming with pride. My teacher had said it was "VERY INTERESTING"...

In my mind, I attributed it to the fact that she was probably having a bad day; yeah, that was it, she was having a bad day. I still remember when my mother said, "Oh, you, poor silly child, your teacher was telling you—in a nice way—that she did not like your masterpiece at all." With no homework needing to be completed that day, Dougie and I met outside. "I'll beat you to the corner," I yelled. "On your mark, get set, go!" It wasn't my legs that got me there first. I would have beaten everyone in my class that day; it would have been simple to even beat my mother that day.

For the remainder of the year, I "skated" through the class I had once loved so dearly. I had decided that it was better for me to be a builder anyway. After all, I knew that I wasn't made to create art. Those words— "you, poor silly child" —were a constant reminder.

After the race, we returned to what we knew best. We focused on building better roads, better towns, and better places to live.

A CHANGE IN THE AIR

THE DAYS GOT SHORTER, AND the autumn chill became more noticeable. Dougie and I still did the things we loved. Hours upon hours, we built and graded roads. Hours upon hours, we wrestled. Hours upon hours, we played the card game "War". We shuffled the deck. Next, we each received three cards face down as the other dealt them. Then, we received another card face up. The person holding the highest face-up card won all the cards dealt that hand. We played until one of us ran out of cards because that allowed one of us to declare victory; we had to have a clear winner. Remember, those were the days of winners and losers.

Dougie and I were very competitive, always trying to win. However, we had one important exception, the work we did when we built roads.

It was a fall day, and we had just finished our homework and a game of War. Dougie was the first to say it, but I was ready to beat him to the corner once again. My victories came more often and more frequently. I knew that I must be getting stronger and faster. A typical boy, I enjoyed rubbing it in when I claimed a victory; in fact, it provided the highlight of my day. "I'll beat you to the corner. On your mark, get set, go!"

THE PROLONGED CHANGE

ABOUT HALF WAY THERE, IT happened. Dougie fell. Suddenly, the victory seemed very hollow. It didn't feel good to win that race. That day, nothing felt right about winning. As he cried out, I didn't have any idea how to help him. He couldn't get his breath. I did the only thing my little mind could; I ran to get my mother. She dropped everything she was doing, and she quickly ran next door to Dougie' house. Dougie's mother and my mother raced down the street. For a very brief moment, a thought crossed my mind—one of them had said "On your mark, get set, go!"

Dougie's mother decided they needed to call a doctor. This was long before you could dial 911 for an emergency. The sequence of events isn't exactly clear. It is hard to put order to the chaos that transpired that day, more than 60 years ago. After our mothers ran to the corner, it seemed like an eternity until something else happened. All of the neighbors converged around my best friend who was still struggling on the ground despite the presence of so many adults. As they tried to catch a glimpse of the little boy, they bumped into each other. Eventually, the silence was broken by the wailing of a siren. Then, there was a second siren and soon, a third. The noise was deafening because I had never heard sirens up close prior to this scary moment. First, a fire truck arrived. It was followed by an ambulance and finally a police car. We all watched helplessly while they lifted my building buddy onto a bed on wheels. It felt like hours until the long, red and white car turned on its siren again and departed.

I really wanted to go with my friend, but I was told that I had to stay home. It would be an understatement to say that I was anxious and upset.

HIGH ANXIETY

MAYBE I SHOULD HAVE LET him win. Maybe we shouldn't have raced that day. Perhaps if I had done something differently that day, Dougie would be okay. I don't remember sleeping that night, but I am sure that I probably did. I just knew that when I woke up that next morning and headed to the bus stop, Dougie would exclaim, "I'll beat you to the corner! On your mark, get set, go," and I would, of course, gladly let him win. Thoughts raced through my mind—just one more time, PLEASE, and it will all be okay...

Dougie and I did not race that next morning. Dougie's mother told me that he was in a hospital because he was very sick. What is a hospital anyway? Why can't I see him? What did it mean that Dougie was very sick? I did not know sickness from a slice of bread. One thought consumed me—he will come home soon, right?

It was the custom for parents to call the school office when one of their children would not be attending school that day. Our teacher told the class that Dougie was sick. She also told us that when it was time for art class, we all could make a picture for Dougie. It was extremely difficult to think about anything except Dougie so I started to plan what I would put on paper for my true best friend.

We would have recess, and then, it would be time for our art class. On that day, I had decided that I was going to make the best drawing ever. My mother would not see it anyway. I drew a set of roads, intersecting with each other. They were the best roads ever captured on paper. It was like I was looking down, just like Dougie and I did at the end of each day.

Again, the art teacher said those dreaded words that I had hoped to never hear again, "That is very interesting! I am sure Dougie will like that picture." It probably would have been better if she had said, "That is terrible. Throw it away." I had given it my very best, but all I got was "That is very interesting." The art class had ended for the day, and I felt terrible. I was facing the fact that my picture was very interesting, but I was worried that Dougie may never see it at all. I worried that it would probably end up in the trash can. The renderings from the class were collected and delivered to Dougie's mother. I really hoped he would at least get to see mine; however, since it was very interesting, I had little hope that he would even catch a glimpse of my drawing.

DOUGIE'S MOTHER AT SCHOOL

SHORTLY AFTER WE STARTED OUR addition and subtraction lesson that day, Dougie's mother entered our classroom. The lesson stopped so we could listen to what she had to say. She shared that Dougie had a disease, and he was very, very sick. Then, she delivered the bad news as she explained that his illness would prevent him from running for now, and perhaps, forever. Furthermore, she told us that his sickness prevented him from breathing like he normally would. She told us to take in a deep breath and blow it out, but she told us not to take another breath for as long as we could. Then, she said that Dougie couldn't take that next breath by himself. She said he required a special machine to help him breathe.

THE MONSTERS ARE HERE! RUN!

DOUGIE'S MOM SHOWED US A picture of this big monster that was made out of metal, and it looked like a tube that had swallowed Dougie. It had taken his entire body; only his head was sticking out and just only on one end. It was horrible. It was true; the monsters are taking the children, one at a time.

Despite what was happening to him, Dougie was still smiling. How could this be? His mother had another photograph, and it showed everything from Dougie's viewpoint. He could look into a mirror that was over his face, when he looked into it, he could see some of the monster den. Next, she shared another photo; it showed what Dougie saw when he looked in the mirror.

There it was—my very interesting drawing; it was front and center. It was the very first thing he could see when he looked into the mirror. My terrible picture was located in a place where Dougie could see it anytime he wanted. Oh! How I wanted to build another road. Oh! How I wanted to have him beat me to the corner! Oh! How I missed him!

THE FINAL RACE

DOUGIE NEVER CAME HOME. I attended my first funeral when I was only seven years old. He wasn't in that horrible, monster, metal tube anymore. Now, he was in a decorated box. My "very interesting" picture was above his head. He was smiling like he always did; the same way he smiled when he said, "I'll beat you to the corner." People were crying, but I knew he was just sleeping. He would come back; I just knew it.

Losing my best friend at age seven was the most devastating thing I had ever experienced. Losing my best friend to a monster was debilitating. I knew I would never have another best friend. As life worked itself out over the years, I have had friends—lots of them—but I have had only one best friend. It took me days—no, weeks— no, months—no, years—no, a lifetime to realize that Dougie, my best friend, was never coming back.

He had something like pneumonia. Complications from the disease Polio took him and kept him away forever.

THE HORSE IS OUT OF THE BARN

ALL OF THE SUDDEN, THERE was a big push for every child to get vaccinated. A new vaccine had been created by a physician in Pennsylvania. All the parents in our city took their children to schools on Saturdays for three consecutive weeks. We stood in line, and I kept searching for Douggie as I waited. We received a sugar cube each Saturday. It required three doses of the vaccine for it to work effectively. Oh! How I wish Dougie was here and able to get this miracle elixir. It would be okay, and then, we could build. The bullies wouldn't be there, and we could race to the corner.

MARCHING FOR DIMES

MY MOTHER VOLUNTEERED FOR THE March of Dimes. She wore a paper hat and carried a cardboard canister. Once a month, for nearly a year, she would take me with her, and we would go from house to house. She used me as a prop while telling each person living in the boxes about Dougie. She would end by saying, "You don't want children like this to die; do you?" She would finish by asking them "How much can you spare to save these poor children?"

I can assure you that she became an expert in making people feel guilty. She honed her skill so well that we felt guilty the rest of her eighty- two years.

She was rewarded as her monthly efforts produced the most dimes collected.

ROTARY, MOM AND DOUGIE

I WAS ATTRACTED TO THE Rotary Club because their motto promotes service above self. My Pastor, who was a member of Rotary, convinced me to join. Over the required time period, I worked through the chairs, and I was finally in line to be president of out club with a term running from July 1, 2010 through June 30, 2011. I have jokingly said that I was in line for the presidency because I had missed a meeting; however, in truth, I was actually looking quite forward to the position. From the international president all the way down to each local president, the leadership is a one-and-done year. In other words, you serve one year, and you are done. Being the President of a Rotary club is like herding a bunch of cats. Just before my term started, the founder of Microsoft, Bill Gates, and his wife, Melinda, announced that their foundation would make a challenge grant for all Rotary clubs that raised up to $200 million dollars for the world wide eradication of polio. Before the year was over, the total dollars offered in the match grant had increased to $225 million.

Each local president picked his local service project and his international service project. I had chosen the very catchy idea of "Pennies for Polio." I chose that because I figured that everyone had a jar of pennies at home. Nobody wants to count pennies. Since the United States was Polio free and had been for years, it would be difficult to generate interest in the worldwide eradication of Polio. However, I thought if we could just capture everyone's penny jar, we could raise a "mile of pennies" to assist in the cause. Knowing that a penny is three quarters of an inch wide, it doesn't take long to complete the math and determine that a mile of pennies is just slightly less than $845. During the year of my presidency, the club delivered and raised more than five miles of pennies. On a second campaign, six years later, the same Rotary club raised almost two and a half miles of pennies.

One million new babies are born in India each month. India, Pakistan, Nigeria and Afghanistan remain the endemic countries. To be removed from the endemic list, a country cannot report any new cases for three consecutive years. In the 2010 – 2011 year, there were 115,000 new cases of Polio diagnosed around the world, and the vast majority of cases came from these four countries.

There's no debate; it is a fact—the vaccine works. By the year 2017, the number of new Polio cases diagnosed throughout the world had fallen to eleven. India was actually removed from the list in 2014. This is a testament to that the vaccine developed by Dr. Jonas Salk, works.

MY EPIPHANY

I WAS NEVER SURE WHY I was interested in raising money to eradicate Polio. During a discussion with my mother, I had mentioned what my Rotary project was. As we talked, I told her that I didn't understand why I felt compelled to help with that particular cause.

During that conversation, she told me the story about Dougie and all that had transpired. Suddenly, in a flash, so many missing pieces of my life fell into place. I now understood why it was so difficult for me to have friends, much less a best friend. Finally, I realized why I found art so distasteful. I understood why I had always felt that it was so important to stop the bullying of our children.

I was not vaccinated until after Dougie passed away, and I still have no idea why Dougie developed Polio, and I didn't. I have no idea why he died at age seven, but I have lived to be almost seventy.

The only thing I do know is that the vaccine works. One dose of vaccine costs a mere 70¢. Just a seventy cent donation will save a life… How much can you give to keep children from all over the world from dying as a result of this horrible, crippling disease?

DOUGIE IS ALIVE

I KNOW ONE MORE THING. Dougie is alive in my mind and in my soul. I think about him every day. His spirit that motivated me to help raise whatever money I am able to help eradicate this terrible disease. How much money can you give to help all the future Dougies' lives?

CPSIA information can be obtained
at www.ICGtesting.com
Printed in the USA
BVHW082321260921
617531BV00001B/65